Jesus, the Catechism, and Me

In faithful conformity with the
Catechism of the Catholic Church

Rev. Robert J. Levis, Ph.D.
Gannon University, Erie, PA

Nihil obstat -
The Most Reverend Donald W. Trautman, STD, SSL
Bishop of Erie

April 11, 1997

ISBN 0-9663761-0-2

Third Printing
Copyright ©1997 Pillar of Faith, Erie PA

Dedicated to the

Blessed Virgin Mary

Queen of Truth

FOREWORD

With his new catechism Jesus, The Catechism, and Me, Father Levis is to be commended for making available to young people a solid ad appealing catechetical resource for the study of their faith. Father Levis draws upon his vast experience in catechistic to make the teachings contained in the new Catechism of the Catholic Church more readily accessible to students in the upper grades. While presenting these teachings in an interesting and understandable way, the author remains faithful to the magisterium of the Church.

This new resource responds to a felt need among those involved in catechetical programs in parishes and schools. For this reason, it is my hope that this work will be a success and find wide usage among those responsible for and participating in such programs. I see in this compendium of the faith also a useful tool for introducing the doctrine of the Church to those adults who are approaching it for the very first time and who may be thinking of converting to Catholicism.

In publishing this work, Father Levis has rendered a valuable service to the Church and to those of our own time seeking the fullness of faith in Jesus Christ through the Gospel and the teaching of the Catholic Church.

Donald W. Trautman, STD, SSL

Bishop of Erie

April 10, 1997

TABLE of CONTENTS

CONTENTS

CONTENTS

CONTENTS

CONTENTS

CONTENTS

CONTENTS

CONTENTS

CONTENTS

CONTENTS

CONTENTS

CONTENTS

CONTENTS

CONTENTS

CONTENTS

CONTENTS

CONTENTS

INTRODUCTION

A quick glance through this little catechetical booklet might raise some eyebrows particularly when one notices the question and answer format used. Most catechetical materials produced throughout the past 40 years avoided the question and answer mode. Notice also the narrative style of the new Catechism of the Catholic Church. One might wonder why we follow a method of presentation seemingly abandoned.

The reason is not a nostalgic and sentimental choice of the style of the Baltimore Catechism. Neither is it a quiet rejection of the findings and conclusions of contemporary catechetical science over the past 50 years. Rather it is a fresh recognition and acceptance of the question and answer mode of teaching recently acknowledged by the natural sciences, military science, business administration, government agencies, technical training, driver education, computer training, etc. The Church has effectively passed on the Faith to generation after generation using this time-tested method. Why not return to a method newly recognized by instructors in many other fields?

Modern catechetics incorporates psychological developmental theory, human experience, and biblical and liturgical findings, with the presentation of the Faith. Decades of scientific and conscientious effort went into this integrating project with the hope that the child would respond to God's revelation with an active, personal, living act of Faith. These attempts did not always result in success. Many programs failed pitifully because of the want of training of the catechetical teachers most of whom were volunteers with a wealth of enthusiasm but a smattering of professional training. Effectively in so many instances, the Faith was somehow confused with the intricacies of this complex method. Sometimes the method became the content. Often more time and energy was spent on psychological development than on belief and revelation. Results were frequently devastating. It is sadly common to read statistics of widespread religious ignorance today.

What we intend with this little booklet is to stress the essentials of the Faith to children of the upper grades in elementary school. It is the work of the Church to teach the truth and the right of children to learn the truth. We have tried to pose precise and brief questions from the text of the new Catechism of the Catholic Church, and to come up with clear, incisive answers. There is no better way to present truth. We think this is sorely needed today.

This is not to say that this booklet was prepared to be committed to memory by children as occurred so frequently in the past. However answers here can easily be occasionally memorized with profit for the rest of the child's life, as Pope John Paul II advised in Catechesi Tradendae.

No parent, teacher, catechist should attempt to catechize anyone today without a firm grasp of the new Catechism of the Catholic Church. It is the most inspired expression of the Catholic Faith since the Catechism of the Council of Trent. There is no other complete catechetical source of teaching on the Creed the sacraments, the commandments, and prayer as is found here. The biblical, liturgical, and patristic evidence for doctrine are replete throughout. Our humble booklet is meant merely as an aide, a summary, a map through this massive text. It must never be used alone and without close dependence on the new Catechism. We envision the catechist with the open Bible and the Catechism before him as he teaches from this booklet. Children trained with this booklet can gradually grow accustomed and familiar with the larger Catechism until it eventually becomes their favored guide in their relation to God and his Church.

The Creed - *We Believe*

We Catholics have a revealed religion. God himself came down to meet us where we are and to tell us things. We respond by believing and professing our Faith in the Creed. The Holy Trinity - Father, Son, and Holy Spirit - revealed the creation of all things in heaven and on earth with us, his greatest creation. But when Adam and Eve fell into sin, God sent his only Son, Jesus Christ, to save us for his Kingdom of Heaven. He suffered crucifixion, died, rose on the third day, and ascended to the right hand of his Father. He sent the Holy Spirit to his Church to enliven it, to spread it throughout the whole world. This is the divine plan of salvation for all. We respond to all God's saving act and truths by believing.

WHAT WE CATHOLICS BELIEVE

Where did I come from?

> I came from God and one day will return to Him. [Catechism 26ff]

Has God revealed Himself to us?

> God spoke to us gradually by stages about Himself and about us. We call this Revelation. [Catechism 51ff]

Did God make any covenant with His People?

> After the fall of Adam and Eve, our first parents, God promised a covenant of salvation, a treaty, an agreement, a pact. He made an everlasting covenant with Noah after the flood. He made a covenant with Abraham who was willing to sacrifice his only son, Isaac. He made a covenant with Moses and revealed the Ten Commandments on top of Mt. Sinai. Finally, God made an everlasting covenant for all through Jesus Christ. Our Savior. [Catechism 54ff]

Part One

What are Scripture and Tradition?

Scripture is God's speech put down in writing under the inspiration of the Holy Spirit.
Tradition transmits this Word of God to the successors of the Apostles who faithfully preserve, explain, and transmit it to all. [Catechism 80ff]

What is the Magisterium of the Church?

The task of interpreting the Word of God in Scripture and Tradition Jesus gave to the bishops in communion with the Pope. This is called the Magisterium. [Catechism 84ff]

What is faith?

Faith is a personal accepting of God who reveals Himself through words and deeds. We believe in only one God: the Father, the Son, and the Holy Spirit. It is a gift from God and necessary for salvation. [Catechism 144ff]

What is the Apostles' Creed?

I believe in God, the Father almighty, creator of heaven and earth. I believe in Jesus Christ, his only Son, our Lord. He was conceived by the power of the Holy Spirit and born of the virgin Mary. He suffered under Pontius Pilate, was crucified, died, and was buried. He descended into hell. On the third day he rose again. He ascended into heaven and is seated at the right hand of the Father. He will come again to judge the living and the dead. I believe in the Holy Spirit, the holy Catholic Church, the communion of saints, the forgiveness of sins, the resurrection of the body, and life everlasting. Amen. [Catechism 166ff]

What is the central mystery of the Christian faith?

The most holy Trinity is the central mystery of the Christian faith. Jesus reveals that He is God's Son, of the same substance as His eternal Father, that He is one and the same God. The Holy Spirit, sent from the Father and the Son, reveals that with them He is one and the same God. By Baptism, we share in the life of the most Blessed Trinity. [Catechism 232ff]

Part One

What do we mean by creation?

Creation is the foundation of all God's work. It is the beginning of the history of salvation in Christ. It explains where I come from and where I am going. God the Holy Trinity created everything out of nothing for His own glory. [Catechism 279ff]

What is divine providence?

Divine providence is the guidance of all creatures to their final end by God's wisdom and love. God does not permit evil unless some good come from it. [Catechism 302ff]

Who are the angels?

Angels are spiritual creatures who always glorify God, who surround Christ their Lord and serve Him. [Catechism 328ff]

Why did God create us?

God created us in His own likeness to serve Him and to rule over all creation. We are meant to become images of Jesus, God's Son made man, to share God's own life. [Catechism 356ff]

Do we have a soul?

> God immediately created a spiritual and immortal soul for each person.
> [Catechism 362ff]

Who were our first parents?

> God created Adam and Eve, our first parents, and placed them in original holiness in paradise.
> [Catechism 369ff]

What do we mean by the Fall?

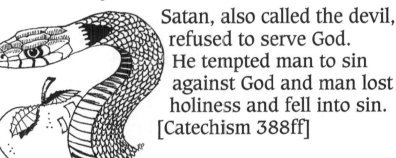

> Satan, also called the devil, refused to serve God.
> He tempted man to sin against God and man lost holiness and fell into sin.
> [Catechism 388ff]

What is original sin?

> Adam and Eve transmitted to their descendents a wounded human nature, deprived of grace. That nature is weakened, inclined toward sin (concupiscence), ignorance, suffering, and death.
> [Catechism 396ff]

(The only human person not conceived in sin was Mary, the Mother of God; this is called the Immaculate Conception.)

Is Christ the remedy for the fall?

Jesus Christ, crucified and risen from the dead, has set us free from sin. He has given us greater blessings than sin has taken from us. That is why the Gospel is called "the Good News." [Catechism 410]

What are the names of Jesus?

The only son of Mary is called Jesus, which means "God saves". He is also called Christ or Messiah which means "the anointed". The Jews anointed the head and hands of their kings, priests, and prophets to set them apart because they had a special job to do.

Jesus is called "Son of God" because he is the only Son of God the Father; he is truly divine, God himself.

Jesus is called "Lord" because he is the center, the master, the king, the purpose of all things. [Catechism 422ff]

What is the Incarnation?

When God the Father decided, he sent his only Son to assume human nature but without losing his divine nature. Jesus is not two persons, but only one divine person with two natures, divine and human. This is the Incarnation. [Catechism 456ff]

Who is the Blessed Virgin Mary?

God chose the Virgin Mary to be the mother of his Son. He preserved her free from all sin from the first moment of her conception in St. Ann to her death. This is the Immaculate Conception. She is truly the Mother of God, mother of the eternal Son of God made man. [Catechism 484ff]

How did the Incarnation happen?

When the Archangel Gabriel told Mary of God's plan and she answered "yes" (Lk. 1:28), Mary conceived Jesus by the power of the Holy Spirit. Jesus had no human father, just a divine Father.

St. Joseph was his foster father, not his real father who was in heaven. Mary remained always a virgin with no other children on earth. She is called the new Eve because she became the mother of all the living by her obedience. [Catechism 494ff]

Why do we call the whole of Christ's life a mystery?

The whole of Christ's life is a sign, a sacrament of his divinity and the salvation of all. His miracles, his talks, his prayer, his love for the poor and the sinner, his suffering and death on the cross, his resurrection - everything points to his divine sonship and his mission of salvation. [Catechism 512ff]

How is Jesus our model?

Jesus calls all men and women to follow him. He promised to live on in them if they live in him. He wanted all to share in his life and death, in his mystery. He wanted his mystery to continue in his whole church till the end of time. He calls all to be one with him so that all can share the fruits of his life and death.

Did Jesus inaugurate the kingdom of heaven?

Jesus inaugurated the kingdom of heaven while he lived on earth. He gathered about himself people who repented and believed his gospel. This gathering is the Church, the beginning and seed of the kingdom. He invited all sinners to the kingdom. It belongs to the poor and the lowly. He gave to Peter the keys to the kingdom. Jesus' triumphal entry into Jerusalem as the Messiah-King was a sign of all this. [Catechism 541ff]

Did Jesus die accidentally?

Jesus' death by crucifixion on Calvary did not happen by chance or accident. Jesus freely delivered himself up to death by the definite plan and knowledge of God. "Christ died for our sins in accordance with the scriptures". 1Cor. 15:3 God saved us because he loved us by dying for our sins. Jesus himself explained the meaning of his life and death in terms of Isaiah's suffering Servant. Mt. 20:28. [Catechism 599ff]

Who is responsible for Jesus' death?

All sinners are responsible for the suffering and death of Jesus. Demons did not crucify Christ, but sinners who delight in their sins. Neither the Jews at the time of Jesus' death, nor the Jews today can be blamed. [Catechism 595]

What were the fruits of Jesus' death?

Jesus atoned for all sins and faults and made satisfaction for them to the Father. He redeemed us all because of his divine nature and as head of all mankind. He ransomed all from punishment. His cross is the only ladder to heaven. [Catechism 606ff]

Did Jesus truly rise from the dead?

The bodily Resurrection of Jesus is the chief truth of our faith. It is an historical fact. The Apostles saw Jesus in his risen state, believed, and witnessed to it around the world. St. Paul wrote that Jesus appeared to more than 500 persons. 1Cor. 15:5. 638ff

Is Jesus' risen body the same as his body before the Resurrection?

In his risen body, Jesus did not return to ordinary earthly life, but passed from the state of death to another life beyond time and space, to the state of glory.

Will good Christians rise from the dead?

The risen Jesus is the principle of our own resurrection from the dead. Jesus, "the first-born from the dead" Col. 1:18 will one day impart new life to our dead bodies. Because Jesus once rose from the grave, we too will live forever body and soul in heaven. [Catechism 648ff]

Where is Jesus bodily today?

Jesus ascended into heaven and is seated at the right hand of the Father. There he intercedes for us assuring us of the permanent outpouring of the Holy Spirit. [Catechism 659ff]

What is the final judgment?

At the end of the world, on Judgment Day, Jesus will come in complete victory of good over evil. He will judge the living and the dead; he will award everyone reward or punishment according to his good or evil deeds. [Catechism 668ff]

Who is the Holy Spirit?

The Holy Spirit is the name of the third Person of the Holy Trinity. He is also called Paraclete, advocate, the Spirit of Truth, consoler.

What are the symbols of the Holy Spirit?

The symbols are water, anointing, fire, cloud, light, a seal, hand, finger, breath, wind, and dove. The church uses these signs and symbols from scripture to explain the action of the Holy Spirit. [Catechism 691ff]

What is the joint mission of Christ and the Holy Spirit?

The Holy Spirit is of the same divine substance as the Father and the Son. He is equally adorable. When the Father sends his Son, the Word of God, he always sends his breath, the Holy Spirit. So the work of Jesus, our savior, and the work of the Holy Spirit are different but inseparable. Jesus Christ is the one seen, but it is the Holy Spirit who reveals him. [Catechism 689ff]

When did Jesus promise the Holy Spirit?

Just before his death, Jesus prayed to his Father for the coming of the Holy Spirit. The Father sent the Spirit in Jesus' name. At the end Jesus breathed the  Holy Spirit on his disciples so that today the mission of Jesus and the Holy Spirit becomes the mission of the Church. [Catechism 727ff]

What happened on Pentecost?

On Pentecost Christ, the Lord, poured out the Holy Spirit in the form of wind and parted tongues of fire on his disciples. On that day the three Persons of the Trinity are fully revealed and the Kingdom of God, life in the Trinity, is open to all Christians. Pentecost begins the time of the Church. [Catechism 731ff]

Part One

What does the Holy Spirit do for us?

The Holy Spirit builds up, animates, and sanctifies the Church. The "first fruits" of the Spirit is the very life of God himself, of the Trinity, which is to love God as God loves himself. The fruits of the Spirit are love, joy, peace, patience, kindness, goodness, faithfulness, gentleness, self-control. (Gal. 5:22-23)

Is the Church the fulfillment of the mission of Christ and the Spirit?

Their mission is completed in the Church, which is the Body of Christ and the Temple of the Holy Spirit. Today the Holy Spirit prepares people to come to Christ, the Spirit manifests the risen Lord to them and opens their minds, he makes present the mystery of Christ to reconcile them, and to bring them into communion with God. [Catechism 737ff]

What is the Church?

The Church is the assembly of all those called by God's Word. It is the gathering together of God's People who are the Body of Christ. The Church is called sheepfold, cultivated field, God's building, mother, new Jerusalem. [Catechism 751ff]

Did God plan a Church?

In the Old Testament, God prepared for the Church, Jesus founded it in his death and Resurrection. The Holy Spirit at Pentecost manifested it, and it will be perfected in the glory of heaven. [Catechism 761ff]

Did Jesus Christ found the Church?

Jesus founded the Church by preaching the promised Kingdom of God. The Church is the mysterious reign of Christ on earth. To build his Church, he chose the Twelve Apostles with Peter as their head. The Church was born from the wounded side of the dead Christ on the cross. [Catechism 763ff]

Is the Church both visible and spiritual?

The Church is the bearer of divine life, yet exists visibly on earth in history. It is the mystical body of Christ yet led by the hierarchy (bishops, priests, deacons). It is both human and divine. Today the Church is in exile but will be perfected in heavenly glory. [Catechism 770ff]

Part One

Is the Church the universal sacrament of salvation?

The Church, like a sacrament, is a sign and instrument of the union of man with God and with others. The Church is Christ's instrument for the salvation of all. The Church is the visible plan of God's love for all humanity. [Catechism 774ff]

What are the characteristics of the Church as People of God?

The People of God are "a chosen race, a royal priesthood, a holy nation". 1 Pet. 2:9
One becomes a member by being born again of water and the Spirit. Jesus the Christ is the messianic Head of this People.

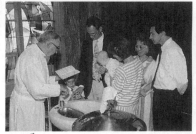

They have the freedom of sons of God since the Holy Spirit dwells in them as in a temple.
Their law is the new commandment of love as Christ loved all.
Their mission is to be the salt of the earth.
Their destiny is the Kingdom of God to its full completion at the end of time. [Catechism 782]

Do the People of God share in Jesus' priesthood,

prophecy, and kingship?

The whole People of God participate in Jesus' anointing by the Holy Spirit as priest, prophet, and king. [Catechism 783ff]

Is there a communion between Jesus and his People?

There is a real and intimate communion between Jesus and his  believers. "Remain in me, as I remain in you. " Jn. 15:4. At his death Jesus sent his Holy Spirit to them. All his followers Jesus calls his body. Jn.6:56 The Church is the Mystical Body of Christ. Jesus is its head, the Church is his bride. Col. 1:18, Jn.3:29
The Holy Spirit makes the Church the temple of the living God.
2 Cor. 6:16 The Spirit is the soul of the Mystical Body, the source of its life and of its riches.
[Catechism 787ff]

Is the Church one?

The Church is one because of its source. Its founder restored the unity of all people in one body. The Church has one soul, the Holy Spirit. She confesses one Lord, one faith, has one Baptism and one hope. She is governed by one Supreme Pontiff and the bishops in communion with him. [Catechism 813ff]

Is the Church holy?

The Church is holy because Christ loved the Church as his bride, gave himself up for her to sanctify her. All her activity is for the sanctification of mankind. The Church is the sinless one but still made up of sinners. In Mary, the Church is already all-holy. [Catechism 823ff]

Is the Church catholic?

Catholic means universal. The Church is catholic because Christ is present in her and so has all the means of salvation. It has the correct and full confession of faith, full sacramental life, and ordained ministry in apostolic succession. The Church is catholic because sent by Christ on a mission to the whole of the human race. She is missionary in her very nature. [Catechism 830ff]

What does the formula "Outside the Church

there is no salvation" mean?

It means that all salvation comes from Christ the Head through the Church which is his Body. The Church is necessary for salvation. Christ is the one Savior and he is present in the Church. If a person knows that the Church is necessary for salvation, founded by Christ, and would refuse either to enter it or to remain in it, he cannot be saved. This is not true if one is ignorant of Christ and his Church. [Catechism 846ff]

Is the Church apostolic?

The Church is apostolic because built on the Twelve Apostles. She teaches infallibly and cannot be destroyed. Christ governs her through Peter and the Apostles present in the Holy Father and the college of bishops.

Does the only Church of Christ subsist

in the Catholic Church?

> The only Church of Christ, one, holy, catholic, and universal, subsists only in the Catholic Church, governed by the magisterium, i.e. the Pope and the college of bishops in communion with him. [Catechism 870]

Who is the pope?

> To lead and shepherd his Church, Christ made a body of men, the Apostles, with Simon whom he renamed Peter, the rock, as head. The bishops and the Pope today are the successors of these men. Jesus entrusted the keys to the Kingdom to Peter. As successor to Peter, the Pope has supreme, full, immediate, and universal power in the Church. He is the Vicar of Christ on earth. [Catechism 874ff]

Who are the bishops of the Church?

> The bishops are the successors of the Apostles. They are authentic teachers of the faith, celebrate the sacred liturgy especially the Eucharist, and guide their Churches. Priests and deacons assist them in these duties. Bishops have no authority unless united with the Pope. [Catechism 883ff]

What is the Magisterium of the Church?

The task of the Magisterium is to prevent the teaching of error to the faithful and to guarantee the truth that frees. Christ endowed his Shepherds, the Pope and the Bishops in communion with him, the chrism of infallibility in faith and morals. When the Pope as supreme pastor and teacher proclaims a doctrine to be of faith or morals he speaks infallibly. When the bishops together with the Pope teach, they teach infallibly, especially in an Ecumenical Council. [Catechism 888ff]

What is a lay man or lay woman?

Lay persons live a life in the secular world and are called by God to be a leaven in that world. They are united to the priesthood of Christ by reason of their Baptism and Confirmation. They all are called to be holy, to be saints, to be witnesses to Christ. Each is a witness and instrument of the mission of the Church. [Catechism 897]

What is the consecrated life?

A life consecrated to God is one in which a person professes the evangelical counsels of poverty, chastity, and obedience in a stable state of life recognized by the Church. [Catechism 934ff]

What is the Communion of Saints?

Communion of saints means the union of holy things and holy persons. It means that what each person suffers and does in Christ bears fruit for everyone. The communion is made up of the faithful on earth, the dead being purified, and the blessed in heaven. God is ever attentive to their prayers. [Catechism 946ff]

Is the Blessed Virgin Mary Mother of the Church?

Mary is not only mother of Christ, she is mother of the members of Christ, the believers in the Church. Her role in the Church is inseparable from her union with Christ and his work. Mary, given by the dying Christ as mother to John, his beloved disciple, was given also as mother to all believers.

Mary was with the Apostles on Pentecost when the Holy Spirit descended on them. Her bodily Assumption into heaven is a participation in her Son's Resurrection as well as the resurrection of other Christians. [Catechism 964ff]

Is Mary our model of faith and charity?

Mary is the preeminent and unique model of faith and charity in the Church. In a perfect way she cooperated by her obedience, faith, hope, and charity in the Lord's work of restoring supernatural life to souls. The Church invokes her help under the titles of Advocate, Helper, Benefactress, and Mediatrix. [Catechism 967ff]

Is devotion to Mary proper to Catholic worship?

From ancient times Mary has been honored as Mother of God. This special devotion differs essentially from the adoration given to Jesus and his Father and the Holy Spirit. Her rosary is called "an epitome of the whole Gospel" and is most highly recommended. The holy Mother of God continues in heaven to be mother of all the members of Christ. [Catechism 971ff]

Why do we have to die?

> We have to die because of original sin which we all inherit from our first parents. Death is the separation of body from soul. If they had not sinned, we would not have to die. Death is the end of earthly life. [Catechism 988ff]

What is the resurrection of the body?

> Just as Jesus rose from the dead and lives forever, the good will live forever with the risen Christ and he will raise them up on the last day. Our physical body will come to life again. [Catechism 988ff]

Will everyone rise again?

> All the dead will rise. The good will rise with a glorified body to new and eternal life, the wicked to judgment on the last day.

Is the Christian today already risen?

> In a certain sense the Christian already participates in the life of the risen Lord. In Baptism the Father raises us up with Jesus. "For to me life is Christ, and death is gain". Phil. 1:21 In Baptism we have already died with Christ. In Eucharist we already belong to the Body of Christ. [Catechism 1002]

What is the particular judgment?

At the very moment of death, each person is judged and either enters into heaven immediately or after purification in Purgatory or immediately into everlasting punishment, hell. [Catechism 1021ff]

What is heaven?

Whoever dies in God's grace live forever with the Holy Trinity. This communion of life and love with God, the Virgin Mary, the angels, and all the saints is called heaven. To live in heaven is to be with Christ. "What eye has not seen, nor ear has not heard, and what has not entered the human heart, what God has prepared for those who love him". 1Cor. 2:9 The contemplation of God in heaven is called the beatific vision. [Catechism 1023ff]

What is Purgatory?

Those who die in God's grace but are still imperfect will eventually live in heaven but first must undergo purification. This purification, entirely different from the punishment of the damned is called Purgatory. The scriptures speak of a cleansing fire. (1:Cor. 3:15)

The Church has always prayed for the dead, urged alms, the gaining of indulgences, and penance for the deceased. [Catechism 1030ff]

What is Hell?

To die in mortal sin without repenting means remaining separated from God forever by one's own free choice. This state of exclusion from God is called hell. Jesus often speaks of "fiery Gehenna" (Mt. 5:22), the "fiery furnace" (Mt.:13:42), "everlasting fire" for all evil doers. The chief punishment of hell is eternal separation from God, in whom alone one can find happiness. God predestines no one to go to hell. [Catechism 1033ff]

What is the Last Judgment?

On the last day, in the presence of Christ come in glory and all his angels, all the dead, the just and the unjust, will be judged and all the good and evil of each will be revealed. This is the Last Judgment when all the nations and history will be judged. God's final justice will be revealed in triumph over all the injustices committed by sinners. [Catechism 1038]

The Seven Sacraments –

We Celebrate

Jesus Christ, the Word made flesh, continued the works of God of the Old Covenant. He made a new covenant sealed with his blood on Calvary which will last through all ages.

The Church celebrates this Paschal mystery without ceasing to let this saving blood flow over us. This is done through the action of the Holy Spirit in the seven sacraments. The Spirit moves, enlivens, encourages, informs the minds and hearts of all believers when they receive each sacrament with loving faith. The most wondrous of all sacraments is the Holy Eucharist where the Spirit fills the believing soul with all the fruits of Jesus' Paschal mystery.

CELEBRATION OF THE CHRISTIAN MYSTERY

What is the Christian liturgy?

The liturgy is the participation of the People of God in the work of God. Through the liturgy Christ, our redeemer continues the work of our redemption in, with, and through the Church. [Catechism 1069ff]

Is God the Father adored in the liturgy?

God the Father is adored as the source and end of all creation and salvation. Here the Church blesses the Father through the Son in the Holy Spirit for all his gifts.

What is Christ's work in the liturgy?

Christ makes his Paschal mystery present and active in the liturgy. Jesus suffered, died, was buried, rose from the dead, and now is seated at the right hand of his Father. This is his Paschal mystery, real historical events that occurred only once, but which will never pass away. All Jesus did is now eternal, is

above time, and is present in every age through the liturgy.
[Catechism 1140ff]
The liturgy not only recalls the events that saved us, but makes them present. The Paschal mystery of Christ is celebrated, but never repeated. [Catechism 1104ff]

Is Christ present in every liturgy?

Christ is always present in the Church, especially in her liturgy. He is present in the priest who celebrates Mass. He is specially present in the consecrated bread and wine (called the species). It is really Christ who baptizes. He is present in the sacred Scriptures read in Church. He is present whenever the Church prays and sings.
[Catechism 1084ff]

Is the Holy Spirit present in the liturgy?

Every liturgical act is an encounter between Christ and his Church. The Holy Spirit prepares the assembly to meet Christ, to make his work present and active by his power, and to make fruitful this communion with Christ.

The Holy Spirit recalls to the assembly all that Christ said and did, all his words and deeds. The Spirit awakens the memory of the Church which inspires thanks and praise. [Catechism 1091ff]

What are the sacraments?

The seven sacraments are effective signs of grace, instituted by Christ by which divine life is dispensed to us. They are Baptism, Confirmation, Eucharist, Penance, Anointing of the Sick, Holy Orders, and Matrimony. They are all actions of Christ and of the Holy Spirit at work in the Church. [Catechism 1113ff]

Are the sacraments necessary for salvation?

The sacraments are necessary for salvation for believers. The Holy Spirit heals and conforms believers to the Son of God. They become partakers in the divine nature in a living union with the only Son, the Savior.

What sacraments confer a seal or character?

Baptism, Confirmation, and Holy Orders confer a sacramental seal or character, by which the Christian

shares in Christ's priesthood and is made a member of the Church. This seal is indelible, it remains forever as a disposition for grace, as a promise of divine protection, and as a vocation to worship and service to the Church. These three sacraments can never be repeated.
[Catechism 1121]

Who celebrates the liturgy?

The whole and entire Christ, head and members, the whole community, celebrates the liturgy.

Our high priest, Christ, celebrates the liturgy continuously in heaven. The liturgy can not be a private function. The community, sharing the common baptismal priesthood of Christ, offer this spiritual sacrifice. Certain members of the community, the bishop and his ordained priests, consecrated by the sacrament of Holy Orders, are the only members set aside to preside at the liturgy.
[Catechism 1136ff]

How is the liturgy celebrated?

The Church employs signs and symbols to express the saving action of Christ the high priest. These include candle, water, fire, washing, anointing, breaking bread, song and music, and the rites of Passover. Just as Jesus used things to express himself in his earthly ministry, to do miracles, so also the Church makes use of visible and common things to express the invisible effects.

What is the liturgy of the Word?

Reading, proclaiming the Scriptures, the word of God is an integral part of the liturgy. The word of God gives life and meaning to all the actions of the celebration. The word and action are inseparable, the action accomplishes what the word signifies. In the liturgy the Holy Spirit awakens faith, gives understanding to the Word, and makes present the wonders of God described in the word.
[Catechism 1153ff]

What are sacred images?

Statues, pictures, sculptures in our homes and churches are intended to awaken faith in the mystery of Christ. He is the one adored and venerated, not his image.

What is the principal day for liturgical celebration?

The chief day for this celebration is the Lord's day, Sunday, the day of Christ's Resurrection. On this day the faithful listen to the word, share in the Eucharist, call to mind the Passion, Resurrection, and glory of Lord Jesus, and to give thanks to God for his own divine life bestowed on them.
[Catechism 1166ff]

What is the liturgical year?

In the course of the year, the Church unfolds the various aspects of the one Paschal mystery. This includes Christ's Incarnation and Nativity through his Ascension to Pentecost. The central feast is always Easter, the "feast of feasts", "the Great Sunday", "the Great Week".

On fixed days, the Church also celebrates the memory of the holy Mother of God, the Apostles, the martyrs, and other saints.

Where is the liturgy celebrated?

In her churches, the Church celebrates, listens to the word of God, prays, and offers the Holy Sacrifice of the Mass. The visible church is the door, the threshold to the Father's house in heaven toward which the people of God are moving. [Catechism 1179ff]

What is Baptism?

Baptism is the sacrament of re-birth through water in the word. It is the washing of rebirth into the new life of Christ and renewal by the Holy Spirit. Without it no one can enter the kingdom of God. Baptism is a bath that purifies, justifies, and sanctifies. It is also called enlightenment, grace, anointing, garment of immortality, seal, most precious gift.
The believer through Baptism enters into communion with Christ's death, is buried with him, and rises with him. [Catechism 1214ff]

How is one baptized?

Baptism is conferred by immersing the person to be baptized or by pouring water on his head while saying, "I baptize you in the name of the Father, and of the Son, and of the Holy Spirit". The pouring of water and saying the words must be done together.

The baptized is then anointed with sacred chrism on the head, perfumed oil consecrated by the bishop, which signifies the gift of the Holy Spirit. The person is clothed in a while garment, a sign that he has put on Christ. A candle, lit from the Easter candle, is given showing that in Christ the baptized is the light of the world. The baptized, if of the age of reason, then receives first Holy Communion, the body and blood of Christ. If still an infant, the child is brought to the altar where the prayer Our Father is recited in his name.
[Catechism 1229]

Who can receive Baptism?

> Every unbaptized person can and should be baptized. The baptizing of infants is an ancient custom in the Church. [Catechism 1246ff]

What is the role of faith in Baptism?

> The faith required for Baptism is not a perfect and mature faith, but a beginning faith. The role of parents and of godfather and godmother is extremely important to nourish the immature faith of the young.

Who can baptize?

> The ordinary minister of Baptism is the bishop and priest and deacon. In case of necessity anyone can baptize, even a non-baptized person, if he has the right intention and pronounces the right words "I baptize you in the name of the Father, and of the Son, and of the Holy Spirit" while pouring the water on the head. [Catechism 1256]

Is Baptism necessary for salvation?

> Baptism is necessary for salvation. Jesus sent his followers to the whole world and commanded them to baptize all. Baptism is necessary

for all who have heard the Gospel and can ask for Baptism. God has bound salvation to the sacrament of Baptism, but he himself is not bound by his sacraments. Martyrs who were not baptized by water are considered baptized by blood and desire.

But any person ignorant of the Gospel who seeks the truth and does the will of God as best he can be saved.

The Church entrusts unbaptized children who have died to the mercy of God. [Catechism 1257ff]

What are the effects of Baptism?

In Baptism all sins are forgiven, original sin, personal sin, and punishment for sin. (Concupiscence, or the tendency to sin, remains, however). By Baptism one becomes a new creation, an adopted son or daughter of God, a partaker in the divine nature, a member of Christ and co-heir with him, and a temple of the Holy Spirit. One is incorporated into the Church, the Body of Christ, and made a sharer in his priesthood. [Catechism 1262ff]

CONFIRMATION

What is the sacrament of Confirmation?

Confirmation is the sacrament that perfects Baptismal grace, that gives the Holy Spirit, roots us more firmly as God's children, and incorporates us into Christ. It binds us more perfectly to the Church and to the spread and defense of the faith. It is the sacrament of Christian maturity. [Catechism 1285ff]

What are the signs of Confirmation?

The anointing with oil signifies a spiritual seal. Oil is a sign of abundance and joy, it cleanses and softens, it strengthens, heals, and comforts. The anointing with sacred chrism in Confirmation is a sign of consecration. The confirmed anointed share more completely the mission of Jesus and the fullness of the Holy Spirit. By this anointing the confirmed receive the mark, the indelible seal of the Holy Spirit, they now totally belong to Christ and his service. One may be confirmed only once. [Catechism 1293ff]

Who is the ordinary minister of the sacrament of Confirmation in the West?

In the West, generally the celebration of Confirmation is reserved to the bishop although, for a grave reason, he may delegate a priest. In the East, infants are confirmed at the time of their Baptism by a priest. The conferral of Confirmation by the bishop brings out best union with the Church, to her origin with the Apostles, and her mission of witnessing to Christ. [Catechism 1297ff]

Who may be confirmed?

One who has attained the age of reason. The person must profess the faith, be in the state of grace. He must have the intention of receiving the sacrament and be prepared to be a witness to Christ in the Church and the world. One must prepare himself to receive this sacrament by a thorough catechesis. He must pray to and study the acts of the Holy Spirit in order better to assume the new duties of an apostolic life. [Catechism 1319]

How is the sacrament conferred?

The bishop anoints the forehead with chrism as he lays hands on the head and says. "Be sealed with the gift of the Holy Spirit".
[Catechism 1300]

What are the effects of Confirmation?

Confirmation increases and deepens baptismal grace.
It roots the person more deeply into divine sonship.

It increases the gifts of the Holy Spirit.
It bonds the person to the Church more securely.
It gives a special strength of the Holy Spirit to spread the faith as a true witness to Christ, to confess boldly the name of Jesus, and never to be ashamed of the Cross.

THE HOLY EUCHARIST

*Why is the Holy Eucharist called the
source and summit of the Christian life?*

The Eucharist is the summit of the Christian life because Christ joins all in his Church with the sacrifice of praise and thanks to his Father which was offered once on Calvary. In the Eucharist he pours out salvation to his Body which is the Church. [Catechism 1324ff]

What is the Eucharist also called?

1. It is called Eucharist because it is thanksgiving to God.

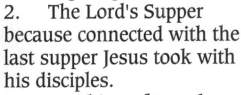

2. The Lord's Supper because connected with the last supper Jesus took with his disciples.

3. Breaking of Bread because Jesus as master of the table used this rite as part of the Jewish meal. By this action Jesus is recognized after his Resurrection.

4. The Assembly because the Eucharist is celebrated with the gathering of the faithful.

5. The Memorial of the Passion

6. The Holy Sacrifice because it makes present the one sacrifice

of Christ and includes the
Church's offering.

7. The Holy and Divine Liturgy
   because it includes all the
   sacred mysteries.

8. The Most Blessed Sacrament
   because it is the Sacrament of
   all Sacraments.

9. Holy Communion because by it
   we unite ourselves to Christ as
   sharers in his Body and Blood.

10. Holy Mass because the final
    dismissal sends us forth to do
    God's will. [Catechism 1328ff]

When did Jesus institute the Eucharist?

At the Last Supper Jesus knew he
was leaving his disciples and going
to his Father. In order never to
depart from them, and to make
them sharers in
his Passover,
Jesus instituted
the Eucharist.
He commanded
his apostles to
celebrate it until
his return,
thereby ordain-
ing them priests.
At this time Jesus
fulfilled the old

Jewish Passover, anticipated his passing over to his Father on Good Friday, and anticipated the final Passover of the Church at the end of the world.

This is why the Mass is always a memorial of Christ and all he did, works made present in the Mass. [Catechism 1337ff]

What is the Jewish Passover?

When the Jews were slaves in Egypt, God rescued them by sending an angel who passed over the houses of the Jews but destroyed the oldest Egyptian sons. God then opened the sea for the Jews to pass through, but closed it on the Egyptians following them. We call this Passover, or paschal event. The Jewish people celebrate it every year.

What are the parts of the Eucharistic celebration?

The Eucharist always includes:

1. proclaiming the Word of God,
2. thanksgiving to God the Father for all his gifts and benefits especially the gift of Jesus,
3. consecration of bread and wine into the body and blood of Christ,

4. holy Communion, receiving the Lord's body and blood. [Catechism 1348ff]

Is the Eucharist a thanksgiving?

The Eucharist is a sacrifice of praise and thanksgiving to the Father for the whole of creation, for all that God made that is good, beautiful, and just. In the Eucharist Christ unites the faithful to this praise and thanks with him, in him, and through him. [Catechism 1356ff]

Is the Eucharist a memorial?

The Eucharist is a memorial of Christ's Passover. It makes present this unique sacrifice. It is not merely a recollection of past events, but a making real and present such events. At every Eucharist the sacrifice of Christ offered once and for all remains ever present and the work of redemption goes on. [Catechism 1362ff]

Part Two

Is the Eucharist a sacrifice?

The sacrifice of the Eucharist is evident from the words of consecration, "This is my body which is given for you" and "This cup which is poured out for you is the New Covenant in my blood". In the Eucharist Christ gives us the very body and blood he gave up on the cross. The Eucharist is a sacrifice because it makes present the sacrifice of the cross, because it is the memorial of that sacrifice and applies its fruits. [Catechism 1362ff]

Is the sacrifice on Calvary the same as the sacrifice of the Eucharist?

It is Christ himself, the eternal high priest, who offers the Eucharistic sacrifice through the ministry of human priests as he offered himself once on Calvary. The victim is the same, on Calvary and on the altar, Jesus Christ. One was bloody, the other, unbloody. [Catechism 1367ff]

Is the Eucharist also the sacrifice of the Church?

The whole Church, the Body of Christ, shares in the offering of her Head. She is offered whole and entire through Christ. Her praise, sufferings, prayers, and work are united with those of Christ and are of new value. In every Eucharist the Pope and the local bishop's named as signs of the unity of the Church. [Catechism 1369ff]

How is Christ present in his Church?

Christ is present:
1. in his scriptural word
2. in the poor, the sick, and imprisoned
3. in all the sacraments and their minister
4. but most specially in the Eucharist.

This last presence in the species is unique. Here the whole Christ is present truly, really, and substantially present. [Catechism 1373ff]

What is transubstantiation?

At the consecration the substance of the bread and wine is changed. The substance of the bread is changed into the sub-stance of Christ's body and the substance of the

wine is changed into the substance of Christ's blood. This is called transubstantiation. The appearance of bread and wine remain but the living and glorious Christ is really and truly present with his Body and Blood, with his soul and divinity. We genuflect and bow before this real presence of Christ, reserve the consecrated hosts in the tabernacle, expose them in solemn veneration, and carry them in procession. [Catechism 1376ff]

What is Holy Communion?

Receiving Holy Communion is receiving Christ himself. Jesus urged us to receive him, ". . . unless you eat the flesh of the Son of man and drink his blood, you do not have life within you". Jn. 6:53
So the altar of the sacrifice becomes the table of the Lord.
[Catechism 1382ff]

How should one prepare for Holy Communion?

One must be in the state of grace to receive Holy Communion. Whoever is aware of being in the state of mortal sin must receive absolution first in the sacrament of Penance or Reconciliation. [Catechism 1385]

How often should one receive Communion?

If one has the proper disposition, one should receive Communion each time one participates in the Mass. The Church obliges everyone to receive Communion at least once a year, if possible, during the Easter season. But the Church highly encourages all to communicate every Sunday and feast day, even daily. [Catechism 1388ff]

What are the fruits of Holy Communion?

1. Holy Communion increases our union with Christ. The Eucharist preserves, increases, and renews the baptismal life of grace.
2. The Eucharist separates us from sin. It cleanses from past sins and preserves us from future sins. It wipes away venial sins. It preserves us from future mortal sins.
3. The Eucharist makes the Church. By it Christ unites all the faithful into one body, the Church. It is the bond of charity.
4. The Eucharist commits us to the poor.

5. The Eucharist is the pledge of glory with Christ. It makes us long for eternal life, unites us to the Church in heaven, to the Blessed Virgin Mary and to all the saints.

PENANCE AND RECONCILIATION

What is this sacrament called?

Penance is called:
1. The sacrament of conversion
2. The sacrament of Penance
3. The sacrament of confession
4. The sacrament of forgiveness
5. The sacrament of Reconciliation.
[Catechism 1424]

Why is this sacrament necessary?

Baptism removes sin but it does not abolish concupiscence, the tendency to sin.
The sinner wounds God's honor and love and his own human dignity. No evil is greater than sin for the Church, the sinner, and the whole world.

Christ constantly called his followers to conversion, to metanoia, to
a complete change of heart. He
called for an end to sin, for a radical
change of one's life. This sacrament
is essential to conversion.
[Catechism 1425]

What is sin?

Sin is an offense against God and a
breaking of communion with him. It
also damages communion with the
Church. [Catechism 1440ff]

Who can forgive sin?

Only God forgives sin. But Christ
gave this power to forgive sins to
his Apostles to act in his name.
Jn. 20:21-23
Christ also gave them the power to
reconcile sinners with the Church.
"I will entrust to you the keys of the
kingdom of heaven. Whatever you
declare bound on earth, shall be
bound in heaven; whatever you
declare loosed on earth, shall be
loosed in heaven" Mt. 16:19
Binding means excluding from the
group, loosing means forgiving and
receiving back to the community.
[Catechism 1441]

Why did Christ institute this sacrament?

Christ instituted the sacrament of Penance for all sinners in his Church, especially for all who fall into serious sin after Baptism. Fathers of the Church have called it the second plank which the sinner may grasp after the shipwreck of sin. [Catechism 1446]

What are the acts of the penitent?

The acts are:

1. Contrition, which is sorrow for sin, hatred for sin, and the resolve not to sin again. When it arises from love of God above all, it is called "perfect" contrition. Perfect contrition remits venial sin, and also mortal sin, if it includes a resolve to confess as soon as possible. "Imperfect" contrition is sorrow because of sin's ugliness, or the fear of hell. By itself it cannot obtain forgiveness of sin but disposes one to sacramental confession. [Catechism 1451ff]

2. Confession of sins. The penitent must carefully examine his conscience, and confess to the

priest all his mortal sins.
The Church commands that one
must confess all mortal sins at
least once a year. One may
never receive Holy Communion
in the state of mortal sin. It is
highly urged to confess venial
sins regularly to keep up our
spiritual defenses. Confession
of mortal sin is the only ordinary means of reconciliation
with God and the Church.
[Catechism 1455ff]

3. Satisfaction. The priest imposes
some acts of satisfaction or
penance to repair the harm
done by sin.
[Catechism 1459ff]

Who is the minister of Penance?

Bishops and priests authorized by
the bishop minister this sacrament.
[Catechism 1461]

What is the "seal" of confession?

The Church binds the priest under
very strict penalties to keep abso-
lutely secret everything he hears in
confession. He can never use this
knowledge. This secret is called
the "seal" of confession.
[Catechism 1467]

What are the effects of this sacrament?

The effects of Penance are:
1. reconciliation with God by the forgiveness of sin
2. reconciliation with the Church
3. forgiveness of the eternal punishment of mortal sin
4. forgiveness of the temporal punishment, wholly or partially, resulting from sin
5. peace and consolation of conscience
6. increase of spiritual strength for the battle of Christian life. [Catechism 1468ff]

What are indulgences?

An indulgence is the forgiveness of the temporal punishment due to sins which have been forgiven. The Church, as minister of redemption, distributes the treasure of Christ and the saints.
Temporal punishment remains after mortal sin has been forgiven. Confession does not remove it. Indulgences may be obtained for oneself, for others, and for the souls in purgatory. [Catechism 1471ff]

How does one receive this sacrament?

1. Pray first to know one's sins and to be sorry for them. Consider sin to be the greatest evil in life. Remember that sin caused the suffering and death of Jesus.
2. Examine one's conscience for any sin of thought, word, or deed against the ten commandments, the precepts of the Church, and one's duties in life.
3. Enter the confessional, make the sign of the Cross, and tell the priest how long since the last confession. Tell your sins humbly and completely.
4. Listen to the advice of the priest and the penance he gives, make an act of contrition, and receive absolution from sin.
5. Leave the confessional and recite or perform your penance.

THE ANOINTING OF THE SICK

What is the sacrament of the Anointing of the Sick?

The sacrament of the Anointing of the Sick confers a special grace on a Christian beginning the danger of death and suffering from old age or illness. It is a sacrament instituted by Christ and referred to in the gospel of Mark (Mk. 6:13) and the Epistle of James (Jas.5:14-5)

Who administers this sacrament?

Only bishops and priests are ministers of the Anointing of the Sick. [Catechism 1516]

How is the sacrament celebrated?

It may be conferred in the family home, hospital, or church, for a single person or a whole group. It can be preceded by the sacrament of Penance and followed by the Eucharist, called "Viaticum". The priest reads from the gospel, in silence lays hands on the sick person, prays, then anoints him on the forehead and hands with oil blessed by the bishop. Each time the person becomes ill again, he may be so anointed. [Catechism 1517]

What are the effects of this sacrament?

The effects of this sacrament are:
1. the uniting of the sick to the passion of Christ for his good and that of the Church

2. courage and strength to endure suffering
3. forgiveness of sins, if the person was not able to receive the sacrament of Penance
4. restoration of health, if helpful for his salvation
5. preparation for passing over to eternal life. [Catechism 1520ff]

SACRAMENT OF HOLY ORDERS

What is Holy Orders?

The sacrament of Holy Orders is the sacrament through which the mission given by Christ to the apostles is carried out until end of time. It includes bishops, priests, and deacons.
[Catechism 1536]

Why is this sacrament called "Orders"?

From ancient times the Church, following Sacred Scripture, but ordination placed certain men into a group, or class, or section, or order. This was a religious and liturgical act, a consecration, a sacrament, a gift of the Holy Spirit, a laying on of hands, a sacred power coming from Christ himself.

Is the whole Church made up of priests?

The whole community of the Church is priestly. Through Baptism all the faithful share in Christ's priesthood. This is called "the common priesthood of the faithful." But the Sacrament of Holy Orders produces the "ministerial priesthood" which serves the whole community. It is essentially different from the common priesthood of the faithful because it confers a sacred power. The ordained priests teach and conduct divine worship and govern the people with the bishop. [Catechism 1546ff]

Does the priest act "in the person of Christ"?

Christ himself is the Head of his Body the Church, high priest of sacrifice, teacher of truth. When the ordained priest acts, it is in the name and person of this same Christ. By ordination the priest acts by the power and in place of Christ, the eternal high priest. He becomes the living image of Jesus. [Catechism 1548ff]

What are the three degrees of Holy Orders?

The three degrees are that of bishops, priests, and deacons. They all are not replacable for the structure of the Church. Without them the Church cannot exist. [Catechism 1554]

What is a bishop?

A bishop receives the fullness of Christ's priesthood. He is the visible head of his diocese. He is a successor of the apostles and member of the whole college (group) of bishops which share the responsibility for the whole Church under the authority of the Pope. [Catechism 1555ff]

What is a priest?

Priests are ordained to be the co-workers of the bishop. They depend on him for the exercise of their pastoral duties and services. The  bishop entrusts them with the responsibility of running a parish or other diocesan duties. They are

consecrated to preach the Gospel,
to shepherd the faithful, and to
celebrate divine worship.
[Catechism 1562ff]

What is a deacon?

Deacons are ordained ministers for
service in the Church. They are not
ministerial priests. They serve in
the ministry of the word, divine
worship, pastoral governing, and
service of charity, all these under
the authority of the bishop.
[Catechism 1569ff]
Since Vatican Council 11, the
Church has brought back the
ancient service of the "permanet
diaconate", which can be conferred
on married men. [Catechism 1571]

How is the sacrament conferred?

Holy Orders is conferred by the
laying on of hands of the bishop,
with a sacred prayer of consecration
asking for the graces of the Holy
Spirit. Ordination to Holy Orders
imprints an indelible character
on the soul. Only the bishop
can ordain to Orders.
[Catechism 1575ff]

Who can be ordained?

> The Church ordains only baptized men who show qualities of service in the priesthood. Church authority alone has the right to call someone to Holy Orders.
>
> In the Latin Church Orders are conferred only on celibate men (unmarried, single) who express their intention of remaining unmarried for the Kingdom of God and the service of the people. [Catechism 1599]

SACRAMENT OF MATRIMONY

What is Matrimony?

> Marriage between man and woman was founded by the Creator. It is naturally ordered for the good of the couple and for the generation and education of children. Christ raised marriage to the dignity of a sacrament. [Catechism 1640ff]

What grace comes with the sacrament of Matrimony?

> Matrimony signifies the union of Christ and the Church. It gives the spouses the grace to love each other

as Christ loves his Church.
It perfects their love, strengthens
their unity, and sanctifies them.
[Catechism 1612ff]

How does Matrimony take place?

The husband and wife
freely give consent mutu-
ally and permanently to
each other to live together
faithfully and fruitfully.
This occurs when they say
"I do". This consent should
be done publicly within the
liturgy, before the priest
or the Church's delegate,
before witnesses, and the
faithful. [Catechism 1625ff]

What are the properties of Matrimony?

Matrimony demands unity between
one man and one woman.
Polygamy (several wives) and
polyandry (several husbands) are
forbidden. Divorce is not permitted,
God seals the bonding. and it must
be open to the birth of children, to
new life. [Catechism 1638ff]

What happens in divorce and remarriage?

> The remarriage of a divorced person breaks the law of Christ. This person is not separated from the Church but cannot receive the Eucharist. They should lead a Christian way of life by educating their children in the faith. [Catechism 1665]

Why is the Christian home called a "domestic church"?

> The Christian home is called a "domestic church" because it is here where the children first receive instruction in the faith. The home also is a community of grace and prayer, a school of Christian virtues and of Christian love. [Catechism 1655ff]

SACRAMENTALS

What are sacramentals?

> Sacramentals are sacred signs instituted by the Church. They prepare Christians to receive the fruit of the sacraments and sanctify different circumstances of life. They resemble the seven sacraments but are not sacraments. The grace that

comes with their use is caused by the prayer of the Church. They prepare one to receive and to cooperate with grace. Some of them are bless-ings of persons, meals, objects, places, churches, altars, holy oils, vessels, vest-ments, bells, etc. Also veneration of relics, visits to holy places, processions, stations of the  cross, religious dances, the rosary of the Blessed Virgin Mary, medals, etc.
The piety of the faithful has always extended the liturgical life of the Church, but has never replaced it. [Catechism 1667ff]

The Ten Commandments -

We Live in Christ

The Old Testament has filled the Christian with memory of God's saving actions. With the Creed in his heart and the Eucharist on his lips, he lives his life in Christ. With light and power from the Holy Spirit, he confronts the world to give witness to Christ. The Christian responds to all God has given him with a life of love for God and neighbor which God demanded in the Old Covenant and Jesus in the New. The commandments are not just ten legal prohibitions but opportunities for the Christian to respond to God's love. With a conscience guided by the Church he lives his earthly life in Christ chosen for eternal happiness.

LIFE IN CHRIST

Should children of God act differently from others?

Since we are children of God and partakers of his divine nature, we must act differently, we must lead a new life worthy of the gospel of Jesus. We must remain dead to sin and alive to God in Christ Jesus. We must not follow the easy road that leads to death, but the narrow and difficult road that leads to everlasting life. [Catechism 1691ff]

What did God create us for?

God created us as images of himself, as human persons with intellect and free will. He ordered us to himself as our final purpose and eternal happiness. [Catechism 1700ff]

What are the Beatitudes?

The Beatitudes are the heart of Jesus' preaching, the summary of the Christian life, and the vocation of the followers of Jesus:
"Blessed are the poor in spirit, for theirs is the kingdom of heaven.

Blessed are they who mourn, for they will be comforted.
Blessed are the meek, for they will inherit the land.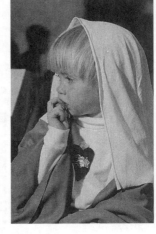
Blessed are they who hunger and thirst for righteousness, for they will be satisfied.
Blessed are the merciful, for they will be shown mercy.
Blessed are the clean of heart, for they will see God.
Blessed are the peacemakers, for they will be called children of God.
Blessed are they who are persecuted for the sake of righteousness, for theirs is the kingdom of heaven.
Blessed are you when they insult you and persecute you and utter every kind of evil against you (falsely) because of me.
Rejoice and be glad, for your reward will be great in heaven.
Matt. 5:3-12

What is the one thing everybody without exception wants?

Every woman and every man wants to be happy. God placed this desire in everyone at creation. [Catechism 1716ff]

What is the one thing that can make people happy?

God alone can make people happy. God alone satisfies. Riches, fame, health, power, possessions, pleasure, human achievement, travel, art, technology, sex - cannot make one happy since they are not the purpose of life. [Catechism 1718ff]

What are the sources of a human action?

Since everyone is free, to act or not, to choose one thing or another, one must determine how to act. Here are the three sources of morality, of goodness or badness of an act:

1. The object of the act. The person sees that this or that thing directs him to his final goal in life or keeps him from it. E.g. prayer, obedience, study, eating, etc. are good. Murder, unjust war, stealing, child abuse are always evil in themselves. They can never be good.

2. Intention or purpose of the act. E.g. helping old people across the street, and minding the baby are good things intended by a brother. Throwing stones and pushing little children around reveal bad intention.

3. Circumstances. These increase or lessen the good or evil of an act. E.g. stealing a dollar from a rich man is not as evil as stealing one from a poor old man.

Every morally good act requires all three sources to be good - the object, the intention, and the circumstances. [Catechism 1750ff]

Does a good intention ever justify a bad action?

No, the end or intention never justifies the evil. E.g. Copying in an exam because one wants to pass is evil. Aborting a baby to prevent the loss of a good name is evil. Some acts are always evil, never good. E.g. unjust killing, slavery. One may not do evil so that some good may result. [Catechism 1755ff]

What is conscience?

Conscience is a judgment of reason, an act of the mind by which one sees the morality of an act. Conscience must be well formed. One must study, read, and use all means to direct his conscience in keeping with the true good of his soul. The holy scriptures are the best means of forming conscience. This is not always easy. [Catechism 1777ff]

Must one always obey a certain conscience?

One must always obey his conscience when he is certain. One must never remain with an ignorant conscience and must correct an erroneous conscience if possible. Ignorance and error are often sinful. [Catechism 1786ff]
One must never do evil so that good may result.

What is virtue?

Virtue is a firm habit to do good. The human virtues are stable dispositions of intellect and will which govern our actions and guide our conduct in line with faith and reason. [Catechism 1803]

What are the four cardinal virtues?

The cardinal virtues, named "cardinal" which means "hinge" since the other virtues pivot on them are: prudence, justice, fortitude, and temperance. [Catechism 1805ff]

Define the cardinal virtues?

Prudence disposes the practical reason to discover the true good and to choose the correct means of attaining it.

Justice disposes the will to give God and neighbor their due.

Fortitude disposes one to be courageous and steady in pursuing the good. Temperance moderates sense pleasure and gives balance in using created things. [Catechism 1805ff]

How can one acquire human virtue?

One can gain virtue by education, by determined acts, and by perseverance, aided by divine grace. Since all are wounded by original sin and his own sins, it is very difficult to become virtuous. All should always ask God for the grace of light and strength, frequent the

sacraments of Penance and
Eucharist, cooperate with the
Holy Spirit. [Catechism 1810ff]

What are the theological virtues?

The theological virtues of faith,
hope, and charity dispose the
Christian to live the divine life with
the Holy Trinity. God himself is their
origin, motive, and object.

By faith we believe
in God, in all he has
revealed, and all that
the Church proposes
for belief.
By hope we firmly
trust God to give us
eternal life and all
the graces to merit it.
By charity we love God himself
above all things and our neighbor
as ourselves for love of God.
Charity is the new commandment of
Christ, it is the fullness of the Law.
Christ asks that we love all, even
our enemies, and especially the
poor. Charity is the greatest of all
the virtues, and, without it, we are
nothing. [Catechism 1812ff]

What are the gifts of the Holy Spirit?

The seven gifts of the Holy Spirit, which complete and perfect the virtues and make the faithful docile in obeying divine inspirations, are:

1. Wisdom
2. Understanding
3. Counsel
4. Fortitude
5. Knowledge
6. Piety
7. Fear of the Lord

What are the fruits of the Holy Spirit?

These fruits are perfections which the Holy Spirit forms in us as the first fruits of eternal glory. The tradition of the Church lists:

1. Charity	7. Generosity
2. Joy	8. Gentleness
3. Peace	9. Faithfulness
4. Patience	10. Modesty
5. Kindness	11. Self-control
6. Goodness	12. Chastity

[Catechism 1830ff]

What is sin?

Sin is an offense, disobedience, revolt against God. It also offends reason, truth, and right conscience.

It is a failure to love God and neighbor caused by wrong attachment to certain things. It ruins man's nature. [Catechism 1849ff]

Name some different kinds of sin?

St. Paul in his Epistle to the Galatians lists: ". . . immorality, impurity, licentiousness, idolatry, sorcery, hatred, rivalry, jealousy, outburst of fury, acts of selfishness, dissensions, factions, occasions of envy, drinking bouts, orgies, and the life." Gal. 5:19-21

What are mortal and venial sins?

Mortal sin is a grave, serious violation of God's law. It turns a person away from God, the purpose of his life. It destroys charity completely. If unrepented, it brings eternal death.
Venial sin offends God in a less serious way and lessens charity although it does not destroy it. One sins venially when he commits a serious sin but without full reflection or full consent. [Catechism 1854ff]

What are the three conditions for a mortal sin?

The three conditions for mortal sin are:

1. Serious matter. E.g. murder, sexual sins, unjust war, blasphemy, etc.
2. Full knowledge. One must be aware of the seriousness of the sin.
3. Full consent of the will. Each person on his own must sufficiently decide to so act.

[Catechism 1857ff]

What can lessen the seriousness of sin?

Factors lessening the seriousness of sin:

1. Real ignorance can diminish or remove guilt.
2. Feelings and emotions, mental disorders can lessen guilt.
3. Malice (hate) can increase guilt of sin. [Catechism 1860]

What are the effects of mortal sin?

Mortal sin:

1. Deprives one of sanctifying grace.
2. If unforgiven, it causes the eternal loss of heaven and the eternal death of hell.

[Catechism 1861]

What are the effects of venial sin?

Venial sin:
1. weakens charity
2. shows a disordered love for things
3. slows down growth in virtue
4. merits temporal punishment
5. slowly disposes toward mortal sin.

But it does not take away sanctifying grace or friendship with God. [Catechism 1863]

What is blasphemy against the Holy Spirit?

This is an eternal sin, unforgivable. If one's heart is so hardened against forgiveness by God, and refuses to accept his mercy by repenting, his sin is eternal. [Catechism 1864]

What are the "capital" sins?

Called capital sins because they cause other sins, they are:

1. pride
2. avarice
3. envy
4. wrath

5. lust
6. gluttony
7. sloth

[Catechism 1866]

What is cooperation in sin?

One has the responsibility for the sins of others when we cooperate in them:

1. by participating voluntarily
2. by ordering, advising, praising, approving
3. by not hindering them when one is obliged to do so
4. by protecting sinners.
   [Catechism 1868]

What is law?

Law is the ordinance of reason for the common good promulgated by one who is in charge of the community.

What is the natural law?

God gives all people a participation in his wisdom to decide what is good, evil, the truth, and error. This natural law is present in the heart of everyone. It expresses the dignity of the human person and is the basis of man's rights and duties. It is unchangeable and cannot be removed from the heart of man. [Catechism 1954ff]

Where can one find the primary principles of the natural law?

> The primary principles of the natural law are expressed in the Ten Commandments. [Catechism 1955]

What is the Old Law?

> The Old Law, the Law of Moses, found in the Old Testament of the bible, is the first stage of revealed law. It is a preparation for the Gospel of the New Testament. [Catechism 1961ff]

What is the New Law or Law of the Gospel?

> The New Law is the perfection of divine law. It is the work of Christ and of the Holy Spirit and is best expressed in the Sermon on the Mount. It fulfills, refines, surpasses and leads the Old Law to perfection. The New Law is a law of love, a law of grace, a law of freedom. [Catechism 1965ff]

Part Three

What does the New Law require?

The New Law of the Gospel requires us to choose between the two ways - the way of nature or the supernatural way of Christ and grace. It is summed up in the Golden Rule "Do to others whatever you would have them do to you." Mt. 7:12. [Catechism 1970]

Does the New Law include the evangelical counsels?

The Law of the Gospel includes the call to holiness expressed in the evangelical counsels of poverty, chastity, and obedience. [Catechism 1973ff]

What is justification?

Justification cleanses from sin and gives us the righteousness of God himself. It includes the forgiveness of sins, sanctification, and the renewal of the inner spiritual life. [Catechism 1987ff] St. Augustine said it is the most excellent work of God's love. It is greater than the creation of the world, than the creation of angels. [Catechism 1994]

Where does justification come from?

The passion and death of Christ on bloody Calvary justified us and now is granted through Baptism. Its goal is the glory of God and the gift of eternal life. [Catechism 1994]

Can one be justified without cooperation?

One must cooperate with God's grace, he must freely assent and accept the Word of God inviting him to conversion and accept the work of the Holy Spirit. [Catechism 1993]

What is grace?

Grace (sometime called "actual") is favor, free and undeserved help that God gives to respond to his call to become his children and to partake in his life.

Grace is supernatural. It depends on God's free initiative alone. It is the life of God himself infused by the Holy Spirit into our soul to heal and sanctify it. One must freely respond to grace, but grace first precedes, prepares, and calls for that response of man.

What is sanctifying grace?

Sanctifying grace is the free gift of God's life to us infused by the Holy Spirit to heal and sanctify. It is habitual, i.e. it remains in the soul. It is a disposition that perfects the soul itself, makes it pleasing to God, and enables it to act and live with God. [Catechism 2000]

What is the difference between actual and sanctifying grace?

Sanctifying or habitual grace is a permanent disposition to live and act with God. Actual grace is passing, and comes either at the beginning of conversion to God or later in the course of sanctification. [Catechism 2000ff]

Should man respond to grace?

Man must respond freely to grace freely given by God. God created man in his own image and likeness, i.e. able to know, love, and choose God as his final end. God has placed in every man a longing desire for himself, but man must freely respond to it. [Catechism 2002]

What are charisms?

Charisms are special graces of the Holy Spirit intended for the common good of the whole Church, e.g. charism of miracles, tongues, prophecy. [Catechism 2003]

What is merit?

God has freely chosen to associate man with the work of grace. Strictly speaking, we have no right to merit since we have received everything from him. God first starts by giving grace, then man follows with his free collaboration. Man's merit is due to God for his good acts proceed in Christ with assistance from the Holy Spirit. Our merits are gifts of God. [Catechism 2006]

Are all called to be saints?

All are called to be perfect, to become saints, to the perfection of charity. This cannot be had without discipline, mortification. "Whoever wishes to come after me must deny himself, take up his cross, and follow me." Mt.16:24 [Catechism 2012ff]

What is the magisterium of the Church?

The Apostles received the solemn command from Christ himself to teach all nations. The Church through this command enjoys the right always to announce moral principles, to judge affairs as they touch upon the salvation of souls. [Catechism 2032]

How is the magisterium exercised?

Ordinarily the magisterium is exercised in preaching and catechesis on the basis of the Ten Commandments which state the principles of everyone's moral life. [Catechism 2032]

What persons belong to the magisterium?

The Pope, who is the Supreme Pontiff, together with the bishops of the world in communion with him make up the magisterium. They are the authentic teachers of the faith on the authority of Christ. The ordinary magisterium of Pope and bishops teach the faithful the truths to be believed and commands of the moral life. [Catechism 2934]

Is this magisterium infallible?

The magisterium of the Church is infallible, i.e. it cannot err in matters of faith and morals. This infallibility extends as far as divine Revelation, to all doctrines and morals without which the truths of faith cannot be preserved or explained. It also extends to the natural law. [Catechism 2035]

What are the precepts of the Church?

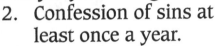

The precepts of the Church are:

1. Attendance at Mass on Sundays and holydays of obligation.

2. Confession of sins at least once a year.
3. Reception of Holy Eucharist during the Easter season.
4. Keeping holy the holy days of obligation.
5. Fast and abstinence from flesh meat on the appointed days.

[Catechism 2041ff]

Name the Ten Commandments.

1. I am the Lord your God; you shall not have strange gods before me.
2. You shall not take the name of the Lord your God in vain.
3. Remember to keep holy the Lord's Day
4. Honor your father and your mother.
5. You shall not kill.
6. You shall not commit adultery.
7. You shall not steal.
8. You shall not bear false witness against your neighbor.
9. You shall not covet your neighbor's wife.
10. You shall not covet your neighbor's goods.

Where did the Ten Commandments come from?

God himself revealed the Ten Commandments or Decalogue to Moses and his people on Mt. Sinai. They are found in the book of Exodus and Deuteronomy. They are the terms of the Covenant made by God with his people. They were written on two stone tablets and deposited in the Ark of the Covenant.

Are all Christians bound to keep the Ten Commandments?

Yes, all Christians must keep the Ten Commandments. The first three concern the love of God, the other seven concern the love of neighbor. These Commandments are an expression of the natural law which applies to all. Although knowable by human reason alone, God revealed them also.

Do all Ten Commandments oblige us?

Yes, the Decalogue binds us seriously to grave obligations. They cannot be changed, they obligate us always and everywhere. They are engraved on the human heart. What God commands is made possible by his grace. ". . . without me you can do nothing. " Jn.15:5

What is the first commandment?

I am the Lord your God: you shall not have strange Gods before me. Jesus said, "You shall love the Lord your God with all your heart, and with all your soul, and with all your mind." Mt.22:37 This commandment calls us to believe in God, hope in him, and love him above all things. [Catechism 2084ff]

*What does the first commandment
oblige us to do?*

> We must adore God, pray to him,
> worship him, and fulfill all
> promises and vows made to
> him. We must have faith, hope,
> and charity toward God.

What is faith?

> Faith, belief in God, is man's first
> obligation. Ignorance of God is the
> chief cause of sin.
> Doubt refuses to believe what God
> and the Church teaches. It may be
> deliberate or not.
> Heresy is the deliberate denial or
> doubt of some truth which must be
> believed.
> Apostasy is the full rejection of the
> faith.
> Schism is the lack of submission
> to the Pope or of communion with
> members of the Church.
> [Catechism 2087ff]

What is hope?

> Hope is the trustful expectation
> of God's blessing and the beatific
> vision of God in heaven.
> Despair is the lack of hope to be
> saved by God or refusal to believe
> in forgiveness of sin.

Presumption is the hope of one saving himself without God or salvation without conversion of heart. [Catechism 2090ff]

What is charity?

Charity is the love of God above all else and of all creatures for him and because of him. Sins against charity are:
1. indifference
2. ingratitude
3. lukewarmness
4. spiritual laziness or sloth, turning down spiritual joy
5. hatred of God
[Catechism 2093ff]

What does religion demand?

The virtue of religion demands:
1. adoration, i.e. to praise and exalt God above all creatures and to humbly submit oneself to him.
2. prayer
3. sacrifice i.e. a sign of adoration, thanks, petition, and communion. The only perfect sacrifice is Christ's sacrifice of the cross and of the Mass.
4. keeping promises and vows.

5. worship of God individually, publicly, and socially. Religion obliges to reveal to ones neighbor truths about God and his one true Church. Christians are called to be lights in the world. [Catechism 2096ff]

Is superstition against the first commandment?

Superstition is departing from the true worship we owe God. It is shown in:

1. idolatry - this makes divine what is not divine. It is adoring what is not God. e.g. satan, power, pleasure, race, ancestors, the state, money, etc.

2. divination - trying to reveal the future. e.g. horoscopes, astrology, palm reading, reading omens and lots, clairvoyance, mediums - all attempt divination. They all dishonor the providence we owe to God.

3. magic and sorcery - trying to tame hidden powers, in order to have powers over others. Magic is sinful if used either to help or harm others. Wearing charms and spiritism are also forbidden. [Catechism 2111ff]

*Is irreligion also against
the first commandment?*

Irreligion is tempting God in words or deeds, sacrilege, and simony:

1.   tempting God - taunting and testing and trying out God's power.
2.   sacrilege - treating unworthily the sacraments, especially the Holy Eucharist, as well as all persons, places, and things dedicated to God.
3.   simony - buying or selling spiritual things.

[Catechism 2118ff]

What is atheism?

Atheism rejects or denies God's existence. It is most common today. Some atheists restrict man to earthly space and time. Others hold that man must do all for himself, by  himself, without a God. Others hold that religion is bad because it distracts man from solving his own earthly problems. [Catechism 2123]

What is agnosticism?

Agnosticism is practical atheism.
The agnostic sometimes posits a
God who cannot reveal himself.
Others neither deny nor admit
God's existence. Others are simply
indifferent to God's existence.
[Catechism 2127ff]

What is the second commandment?

You shall not take the name of the
Lord your God in vain.
Since the name of the Lord is most
holy, one must respect it. We must
use the name only to bless, praise,
and glorify it. [Catechism 2142ff]

What does the second commandment forbid?

It forbids every improper use of
God's name.
Blasphemy is the offensive use of
the name of God, of Jesus Christ, of
the Virgin Mary, of the saints, and
of all sacred things.
Blasphemy is a word of hatred,
or defiance against God.
Being unfaithful to promises
made in God's name breaks this
commandment.
Perjury is making a promise under
oath without the intention of keeping it; it is a grave sin against God.
[Catechism 2152ff]

Is every Christian's name sacred?

Yes, God calls each one by his own name, a name given at the time of Baptism. It should always be a Christian name, the name of a great saint or disciple of Jesus. One keeps that name for eternity. [Catechism 2156ff]

How should one begin his day?

On arising, one should sign himself with the sign of the cross and say, "In the name of the Father, and of the Son, and of the Holy Spirit." [Catechism 2157]

What is the third commandment?

Remember to keep holy the Lord's Day. The sabbath of the Old Testament, the seventh day of the Jewish week, Christians have replaced with Sunday, the first day of the week. [Catechism 2168ff]

Why did Christians change from sabbath to Sunday?

Christians celebrate on Sunday because Christ rose from the dead on Sunday, the first day of the week. Sunday represents a new creation begun with his Resurrection. Sunday represents our eternal rest in heaven with God. [Catechism 2175]

Part Three

What is the most important holy day of obligation in the Church?

 Sunday is the most important holy day in the universal Church. From the days of the Apostles, Christians gathered together for the Eucharist. All Catholics must participate in the Mass every Sunday and holy day of obligation. Unless excused for a serious reason, one commits a mortal sin if he misses Sunday Mass deliberately. [Catechism 2180ff]

How should a Catholic observe Sunday?

The Catholic on Sunday and other holy days of obligation should not do heavy manual work, or do business tasks that interfere with the worship they owe God. Nor should they make heavy demands on others that would hinder them from keeping Sunday holy. [Catechism 2184ff]

Name some good works to be done on Sunday.

Catholics should relax their mind and body on Sunday. It is an excellent day for prayer and meditation, for silence and reflection. They should take special care of the sick

and elderly on this day. They
should cultivate family ties carefully
on this great day. In pagan coun-
tries where the Sunday observance
is ignored, Catholics must work the
harder to defend their tradition.
[Catechism 2185ff]

What is the fourth commandment?

Honor your father
and your mother.
God wants all to
honor him and,
after him, our
parents and
guardians. God
promised a long life to those who
keep this commandment. Ex.20:12

What is a family?

Marriage and the family are ordered
to the good of mother and father
and to the birth and education of
children. A family is only made by
parents and their children. The
family is the original cell of social
life. It initiates one into the social
world of moral values, freedom, and
persons.
A Christian family is called a
"domestic church" since it is a
privileged community of faith,
hope, and love. [Catechism 2201ff]

*What are the duties of children
toward their parents?*

Children must:
1. respect their parents out of gratitude
2. obey their parents humbly. They must also obey teachers and all those to whom their parents have entrusted them
3. as much as possible, grown children should assist parents who are old, sick, lonely, or distressed
4. respect for their brothers and sisters
5. have gratitude toward all who helped them in the baptismal life of faith - parents, grandparents, godparents, sisters and brothers, pastors, catechists, friends.
6. when grown and adult, and with the advice of their parents, children have the right and duty of selecting their own profession and state of life. [Catechism 2214ff]

What are the duties of parents?

Parents have the following duties:
1. the first right and duty to educate their children, which can never be taken from them

2. to regard their children as children of God and as human persons
3. to create a wholesome home with tenderness, forgiveness, respect, fidelity, and service are the rule.

4. to evangelize their children in the mysteries of the faith of which they are the first heralds. To teach them to follow Jesus from the earliest years of the children.

5. to provide for all the spiritual and physical needs of the children
6. to choose a school for their children. This is fundamental. [Catechism 2221ff]

What are some of the fundamental duties of civil society toward the family?

Public authority is obliged to respect the fundamental rights of the human person and the exercise of his freedom. Citizens are not obliged morally to obey the laws of civil society which are immoral. Without the light of the Gospel, civil society easily becomes totalitarian. [Catechism 2234ff]

What is the fifth commandment?

You shall not kill is the fifth commandment.

Every human life is sacred, made in the image and likeness of God, from the first moment of conception until death. God alone is the Lord of life. No one can claim for himself the right to destroy an innocent human being. [Catechism 2258]

What is homicide?

Directly killing a person is homicide and is a grave sin that cries out to heaven. Killing of babies (infanticide), of family members are specially grave sins. The fifth commandment also forbids the indirect taking of another's life. If the killing is not intended, one is not guilty of murder, but still is guilty of serious sin because of carelessness and lack of attention and concern. [Catechism 2268ff]

Is direct abortion a mortal sin?

From its conception, from the first moment of its existence, the infant has the right to life. Directly wanted abortion is gravely sinful always. This teaching is unchangeable. [Catechism 2276ff]

Can one cooperate in an abortion?

Direct cooperation in an abortion is a mortal sin to which the Church adds a canonical excommunication. The Church does this to stress the horrible crime committed, not to limit her mercy and forgiveness. This excommunication also is applied to the doctor, nurse, friends, - anyone who directly assists in the abortion. [Catechism 2270]

Is euthanasia forbidden?

Direct euthanasia, ending the life of the elderly, handi-capped, sick, or dying persons is a mortal sin. Omit-ting some service intentionally which results in the death of the ill is murder, mortal

sin, seriously contrary to God's law.
Seriously ill patients must always
be given ordinary care to maintain
their life; but extraordinary care is
not required to keep them alive.
[Catechism 2276ff]

Is suicide sinful?

Suicide is seriously sinful since it
opposes justice, hope, and charity.
It is contrary to the love of self
and the love of God. It offends the
family, friends, and nation to which
we are indebted.
Helping another to suicide is
 seriously sinful.
Serious mental and emotional
illness, fear of suffering can
diminish the guilt of suicide.
[Catechism 2280]

Is self-defense murder?

One can always legitimately defend
oneself even if the attacker is killed.
This is not murder nor forbidden
by the fifth commandment.
Defense is a right and a grave
duty for all who have the obligation
to defend the lives of others.
[Catechism 2263ff]

Does the fifth commandment
forbid scandal?

Scandal is an attitude or action which leads another to do evil. It is forbidden by the fifth commandment. It is a mortal sin if the other is drawn into serious sin. One who gives scandal draws another into spiritual death. Scandal can come by laws, opinions, fashions, etc. The scandal-giver is responsible for the sin committed by another. [Catechism 2284ff]

Is it sinful to harm one's health?

One must avoid any excess in the use of food, alcohol, tobacco, or medicine.
We sin when we endanger our health or that of others by speeding. The use of recreational drugs is a grave sin. Drug dealing is a serious scandal.

The Christian must avoid excessive worship of the body, as in sports. [Catechism 2288ff]

Is anger permitted?

Anger is a mortal sin if it rises to the point of desire to kill or wound another. It is sinful deliberately to hate another.

*What conditions are necessary
for a just war?*

War and the arms race are man's
great calamities and are to be
avoided at all costs. Just war
is permitted under these four
conditions:
1. There must be reasonable
    chance of success.
2. All peaceful means have failed.
3. The losses inflicted by the en-
    emy must be long-lasting and
    very serious.
4. The harm coming from war
    must not be greater than
    the present harm.
    [Catechism 2307ff]

What is the sixth commandment?

You shall not commit adultery.
God created man and woman, he
blessed them and told them to
multiply. Gen.1:28
The whole human race is either
male or female. While each is equal
to the other, they are different, each
is a person, and one is a mutual
filling out of the other. The happiness of a couple and of all people
depends partly on how the two
sexes interact. [Catechism 2331ff]

What is chastity?

Chastity is a moral virtue by which sex is incorporated well into one's bodily and spiritual life. Jesus Christ is the Christian's model of chastity.

Chastity is a virtue which controls one's sexual impulses, which dignifies one in gaining such control. It is a virtue which collects all ones powers and unites them. Chastity is part of the moral virtue of temperance. Gaining chastity is a life-long effort demanding penance and self-discipline. It is specially hard to master during childhood and adolescence.
[Catechism 2337ff]

Must every one be chaste?

Yes, all Christians especially are called to chastity. Gal. 3:27 One must practice chastity in his particular state of life:

1. consecrated celibates and those with vows of chastity - give themselves to God alone

2. married people - live chastely
    within marriage
3. single people - live chastely
    without a spouse
4. those engaged to be married -
    live chastely and reserve sexual
    activity until the blessed mar-
    riage vows. [Catechism 2348ff]

What are the sins against chastity?

Sins against chastity are:
1. lust - the disordered yearning
    for sex pleasure
2. masturbation - wilful use of
    genital organs for pleasure.
    Use of sex faculties outside of
    marriage is seriously opposed
    to the purpose of these facul-
    ties. Masturbation is a gravely
    disordered act. Its sinfulness
    depends on immaturity, habit,
    anxiety and other psychological
    factors which might lessen
    guilt.
3. fornication - sexual union
    between an unmarried man
    and an unmarried woman. It is
    a mortal sin, contrary to their
    dignity and the purposes of
    marriage.

4. pornography - displays sex activity to the public for the purpose of pleasure and profit. It is a perversion of the marriage act, does grave harm to the actors, the public, the publishers. It is a mortal sin to buy and look at such material.

5. prostitution - sex for pay is a great social disease. It reduces the person to an instrument of pleasure. While it often involves women, it may involve men, children, and adolescents. It is always seriously sinful unless one is forced to engage in it.

6. rape - is the forceful violation of one's sexual privacy. It is a mortal sin against justice and charity. Rape is an intrinsically evil act. It may well injure the victim for life.
[Catechism 2351ff]

Is homosexuality sinful?

Homosexuality is same-sex activity. Scripture forbids it, (Gen.19:1-29; Rom.1:24-27;

1Cor.6:10; 1Tim.1:10).
The Church has always condemned
it as intrinsically disordered and
against the natural law.
Homosexual persons still are called
to be chaste and can be pure
by prayer and the use of the
sacraments. [Catechism 2357]

What are the ends or purpose of marriage?

The mutual good of husband and
wife and the transmission of new
life are the purposes of marriage.
[Catechism 2363]

Can a Christian marriage be dissolved?

When the spouses give their total
consent to the marriage, it cannot
be dissolved
since they be-
come no longer
two, but one
flesh. Just as
Christ the groom
cannot leave his

Church, so also one spouse cannot
leave the other. [Catechism 2364]

Must every conjugal act be open to life?

Yes, every sexual act of the
husband and wife must be open to
the transmission of life. No person

can separate the ends of marriage from one another - love and the generation and education of children - since they are so ordered by God himself. [Catechism 2366ff]

May spouses space their children?

Yes, spouses may space children provided they are not selfish but responsible, and act morally. Morality is not determined by their intention alone. They may not use artificial contraception or sterilization which are intrinsically evil. They may use natural family planning , a system in keeping with objective morality and approved by the Church. [Catechism 2370]

What is the supreme gift of marriage?

A child is the supreme gift of marriage. [Catechism 2378]

What is adultery?

Adultery is sexual unfaithfulness of one spouse or both in marriage. Christianity always forbids adultery. Mt.5:32; Mt. 19:6; Mk.10:11; 1Cor.6:9-10.

Adultery breaks the commitment in marriage, injures the covenant of the spouses, and threatens the family and children. [Catechism 2380ff]

What is divorce?

Divorce is the dissolution of marriage. It is against the natural law, injures the saving covenant with God which marriage signifies. Remarriage after divorce is even worse. Jesus forbade divorce. Mt.5:31-32; 19:3-9; Mk.10:9; Lk.16:18; 1Cor.7:10. [Catechism 2382ff]

Divorce brings chaos into the family and society. It causes grave harm to the abandoned spouse and children. It spreads like contagious plague in society. One spouse can legitimately separate from another without breaking the marriage bond. In these divorces there is an innocent spouse who, faithful to the marital promises, was unjustly abandoned. [Catechism 2382ff]

Is polygamy permitted the Christian?

Polygamy permits a man to have many wives. It is an immoral situation against God's original plan and the dignity of the persons involved. [Catechism 2387]

What is incest?

Incest is sexual union between relatives or in-laws. It is a mortal sin. 1Cor. 5:1,4-5
All sexual abuse done by adults with children under their care is also gravely sinful.
[Catechism 2388ff]

What is free union and trial marriage?

In free union a man and woman live together without marriage. It is gravely immoral because it offends the dignity of marriage, destroys the family, and weakens fidelity.
[Catechism 2390]
Trial marriage is the union of two persons who intend to marry later. It is immoral since it violates human love which demands the total gift of self to each other.
[Catechism 2391]

What is the seventh commandment?

You shall not steal.
(Ex,20:15)
It commands justice and charity over earthly goods and labor.
[Catechism 2402ff]

Do people have a right to private property?

Yes, one has the right to own and dispose of property. But this right must never interfere with the prior and universal gift of God of the whole earth to the whole of mankind.

Is theft forbidden?

The seventh commandment forbids theft, the taking of another's property against the owner's will. Also forbidden is the keeping of things loaned or lost, business fraud, unjust wages, unjust forcing up of prices. [Catechism 2409ff]

What is restitution?

Justice requires returning stolen property to the rightful owner. This is called restitution. [Catechism 2412]

Does this commandment forbid slavery?

This commandment forbids the enslaving of any person for any reason. No human person may ever be bought or sold or exchanged like goods. [Catechism 2414]

Must we show kindness to animals?

God has given animals for man's use and enjoyment; they must always be treated with kindness. They must not suffer or die needlessly. Money should not be spent on them which ought to be spent on human suffering. Medical and scientific experimentation on animals is moral, provided it is reasonable. [Catechism 2415ff]

Can the Church interfere in economic and social matters?

The Church has a right to make judgments in these matters when the fundamental rights of the person or the salvation of souls is at stake. The social teaching of the Church provides principles and guidelines for reflection and action. She forbids profit alone as the final end of man. She forbids totalitarian and atheistic systems where man is reduced to an object. She criticizes excessive individualism and befriends human labor. [Catechism 2419ff]

*What does the Church teach about
the great imbalance between the
very rich and the very poor?*

The Church teaches that the very rich must share some of their wealth with the very poor. In doing this they are not giving a gift but actually giving the poor what they already own. Everyone without exception has a right to share in the wealth of the world for his own and the livelihood of his family. The Gospel requires all to share what they have, especially with the poor. [Catechism 2426ff]

What are the corporal works of mercy?

The corporal works of mercy are feeding the hungry, sheltering the home-less, clothing the naked, visiting the sick and imprisoned, and burying the dead. Giving alms to the poor is a great work of justice. Helping the poor is a preferential duty of all Christians. [Catechism 2443]

What is the eighth commandment?

You shall not bear false witness against your neighbor. Ex.20:16 Since Jesus is the truth (Jn.1:14), all his followers must live and act truthfully. Truth is sincerity in action and speech. Society is impossible without truth. [Catechism 2464ff]

Must Christians always witness to the truth?

All Christians have the duty of witnessing to the truth of the Gospel by their lives and their words. Martyrdom is the supreme witness to truth. [Catechism 2473]

What are the sins against truth?

Sins against truth are:
1. False witness and perjury. Telling a lie in court is false witness; under oath, it is perjury and is gravely sinful.
2. Rash judgment - assuming without basis moral faults of another. It sins against justice and charity.
3. Detraction - revealing without reason the moral faults to one unacquainted with the accused. Also a sin against justice and charity.

4. Calumny -lying about the faults of another.
5. Flattery - wrongful praise and admiration for one doing sinful acts. It can be a serious sin when it helps the sinner to do evil.
6. Boasting - bragging with the purpose of belittling another's character.
7. Lying - speaking falsely with the intention of deceiving. Jesus described lying as the work of the devil. Jn.8:44 Lying becomes a mortal sin when it does serious injury to another.
   Every sin against justice and charity must be repaired. Not to repair damage to another's reputation is a sin.
   [Catechism 2475ff]

Must secrets be preserved?

No one is bound to tell the truth to one who has no right to know the truth. E.g. the right to privacy, the safety of others, and the common good are reasons for keeping safety of others, and the common good are reasons for keeping silence about truth.

The seal of the confessional seriously binds the priest always in every case not to reveal the secrets told him in the sacrament of Reconciliation.

Professional secrets, e.g. held by those in politics, soldiers, doctors, lawyers, must not be revealed except when grave injury would result to several if not revealed. [Catechism 2488ff]

Do people have the right to truth in the communications media?

Yes, all have the right to be informed in justice, truth, and freedom. [Catechism 2493ff]

What is the ninth commandment?

You shall not covet your neighbor's house; you shall not covet your neighbor's wife, or his manservant, or his maidservant, or his ox, or his ass, or anything that is your neighbor's. Ex,20:17

What does this commandment demand?

The ninth commandment demands purity of heart. "Blessed are the clean of heart, for they will see God." Mt.5:8 This commandment demands internal purity of mind and will.

To covet another person's wife or husband is to desire to have sexual relations with that person. Jesus said, ". . . that everyone who looks at a woman with lust has already committed adultery with her in his heart." Mt.5:28

What is chastity?

Chastity is a virtue by which a person controls sexual desires. It is a difficult virtue to practice.

How can one be pure in heart?

One can be pure in heart by:
1. the gift and virtue of chastity
2. purity of intention, fixing one's goal on God
3. purity of vision, by controlling one's feelings and imagination, by quick refusal of impure thoughts

4.   prayer, for without prayer chastity is impossible. Prayer to the most pure Immaculate Virgin and Mother of God is most effective. [Catechism 2520]

Does modesty protect chastity?

Modesty is decency in clothing, speech, and actions. It protects against lurid advertisements in the media. It protects against the fascination of alluring fashions. [Catechism 2522]

What is the tenth commandment?

You shall not covet your neighbor's house. . . . nor anything else that belongs to him. Ex.20:17

What does this commandment forbid?

It forbids greed and avarice, the passion for money and riches. It forbids envy which is one of the seven capital sins. It is sadness at the sight of another's goods and the desire to obtain them, even unjustly. If one wishes serious harm to another, it is a serious sin.

What is the proper use of things?

To enter the Kingdom of Heaven, Jesus asks all to prefer him to riches and to consider wealth a great risk. The first Beatitude is "Blessed are the poor in spirit" Mt. 5:3 ". . . everyone of you who does not renounce all his possessions cannot be my disciple." Lk.14:33 Detachment from riches is necessary for all Christians.
[Catechism 2544ff]

We Pray

We profess our Faith in the Creed. We celebrate it in the sacraments. We live an earthly life in Christ enlivened by the Holy Spirit. This mystery of belief, celebration, and living in a dynamic union with the living God is prayer. Whenever we decide to pray, to seek God in prayer, God has first sought us. He thirsts for us and wants us to thirst for him. Prayer must come from a humble heart and not from busy lips. It is a living communion of the believer with the living God.

CHRISTIAN PRAYER

What is prayer?

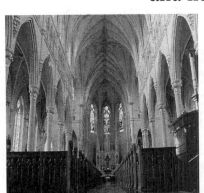

Prayer is the raising of one's mind and heart to God or the requesting of good things from God, St. John Damascene defines prayer. [Catechism 2559] Prayer is one of God's wonderful gifts, often called a thirst for God. God first thirsts for you that you may thirst for him. Whenever you pray, God has first called you to pray. [Catechism 2559ff]

Is the whole Bible a book of prayer?

Yes. Abraham and Jacob prayed for faith and trust in God's love for them. Moses constantly begged God to forgive the sins of the people of Israel. The Israelites loved to pray in the Temple of Jerusalem before the ark of the covenant. All the prophets, like Elizah, called the people to pray and do penance. The 150 Psalms are perfect examples of prayer in the Old Testament. The

Church today makes them central to its own prayer.
[Catechism 2568ff]

Did Jesus pray?

Of course. Jesus was always praying. He is the perfect model of prayer. With perfect confidence, Jesus prayed always to do his Father's will.
He teaches us how to pray with a pure heart. He teaches us to pray boldly with confidence that what we ask for we will receive. He wants us always to pray in the name of Jesus. St. Augustine wrote that Jesus prays for us as priest, prays in us as Head, and is prayed to by us as God. [Catechism 2616ff]

Did the Blessed Virgin pray?

Yes, and the Church today loves to pray in union with Mary because she is the Mother of God. Before Jesus died on Calvary, he gave his mother to all of us as our mother too. When the angel Gabriel told her

of God's plans for her, she answered, ". . . I am the handmaid of the Lord. May it be done to me according to your word." Lk.1:38 The Magnificat or Canticle of Mary is said every day in the official prayer of the Church. (Lk.1:46ff) The Rosary is a private prayer highly approved by the Church. [Catechism 2617]

What are the Church's basic forms of prayer?

The Holy Spirit has instructed the Church in five forms of prayer:

1. blessing - we are all blessed by God's gifts first and respond by blessing God
2. petition - in our needs, we ask God's help, especially to forgive sin
3. intercession - we ask God, not for ourselves, but for another
4. thanksgiving - we thank God for all he has done
5. praise - we give glory to God for his own sake just because he exists. [Catechism 2623ff]

What are the wellsprings of prayer?

There are several springs of prayer where the Holy Spirit dwells to share Christ with us. They are the sacred scriptures, the sacraments especially Holy Eucharist, and the theological virtues of faith, hope, and charity. [Catechism 2652ff]

Should prayer always be in the name of Jesus?

We have entrance to God the Father only through the name of Jesus. But we call on the Holy Spirit to teach us prayer since he introduces us to Jesus. The Church loves to pray in communion with the Blessed Virgin Mary since she is the Mother of the Church and with Christ our greatest intercessor. [Catechism 2663ff]

Where are the best places to pray?

The church building, monasteries, pilgrimage spots, and especially the family home. The Christian family is the nursery for prayer. Parents should teach their children their first prayers at home. [Catechism 2685ff]

Name three differing kinds of prayer.

Three different expressions of prayer are:
1. vocal prayer - speaks to God with words from the heart

2.   meditation - a deepening of faith through the use of imagination, emotions, and desire.

3.   contemplation - a silent, loving gaze of faith fixed on Jesus. [Catechism 2700ff]

Is it difficult to pray?

It is hard to pray. It demands a fight with ourselves as well as with the devil.

Some children do not know even what prayer is. Others don't take time to pray. Others are quickly discouraged when God doesn't answer their prayer immediately. It is a battle both to learn to pray and to continue praying.

Distractions during prayer are very common. To pray well one must be humble, trust in God, and not quit. If one lives according to the Gospel, in the spirit of Jesus, he will pray well. But if one lives a selfish and worldly life, he will pray badly or not at all. One cannot separate a good Christian life from prayer. [Catechism 2725ff]

PRAYERS

Our Father

Our Father, who art in heaven, hallowed be thy name, thy kingdom come, thy will be done on earth as it is in heaven. Give us this day our daily bread and forgive us our trespasses as we forgive those who trespass against us. Lead us not into temptation but deliver us from evil. Amen.

Hail Mary

Hail Mary, full of Grace, the Lord is with thee; blessed are thou among women and blessed is the fruit of thy womb, Jesus. Holy Mary, Mother of God, pray for us sinners, now and at the hour of our death. Amen.

Glory be to the Father

Glory be to the Father and to the Son and to the Holy Spirit, as it was in the beginning, is now, and ever shall be, world without end. Amen.

The Apostles' Creed

I believe in God, the Father almighty, Creator of heaven and earth. And in Jesus Christ, his only Son, our Lord: who was conceived by the Holy Spirit, born of the Virgin Mary, suffered under Pontius Pilate, was crucified; died, and was buried. He descended into hell, the third day he arose again from the dead; he ascended into heaven, sits at the right hand of God the Father almighty; from thence he shall come to judge the living and the dead. I believe in the Holy Spirit, the holy Catholic Church, the Communion of Saints, the forgiveness of sins, the resurrection of the body, and life everlasting. Amen.

Hail Holy Queen

Hail, Holy Queen, Mother of Mercy, our life, our sweetness, and our hope. To you do we cry, poor banished children of Eve. To you do we send up our sighs, mourning and weeping in this valley of tears. Turn, then, most gracious advocate, your eyes of mercy towards us. And after this our exile, show unto us the blessed fruit of your womb, Jesus. O clement, O loving, O sweet Virgin Mary.

V. Pray for us, O holy Mother of God.
R. That we may be made worthy of the promises of Christ.

Angel of God

Angel of God, my guardian dear,
To whom his love commits me here,
Ever this day be at my side,
To light and guard, to rule and guide.
Amen.

Eternal Rest

Eternal rest grant unto them, O Lord, and may perpetual light shine upon them.
May they rest in peace. Amen.

Act of Faith

O my God! I firmly believe that you are one God in three divine persons, the Father, the Son, and the Holy Spirit. I believe that your divine son became man, and died for our sins, and that he will come to judge the living and the dead. I believe these and all the truths which the holy Catholic Church teaches, because you have revealed them, who can neither deceive nor be deceived. Amen.

Act of Hope

O my God! Relying on your infinite goodness and promises, I hope to obtain pardon of my sins, the help of your grace, and life everlasting through the merits of Jesus Christ, my Lord and Redeemer. Amen.

Act of Love

O my God! I love you above all things, with my whole heart and soul, because you are all good and worthy of all love. I love my neighbor as myself for love of you. I forgive all who have injured me, and ask pardon of all whom I have injured. Amen.

Act of Contrition

O my God! I am heartily sorry for having offended you, and I detest all my sins, because I dread the loss of heaven and the pains of hell, but most of all because they offend you, my God, who are all good and deserving of all my love. I firmly resolve, with the help of your grace, to confess my sins, to do penance and to amend my life. Amen.

V. The angel of the Lord declared unto Mary,

R. And she conceived by the Holy' Spirit.

Hail Mary, etc.

V. Behold the handmaid of the Lord.

R. Be it done unto me according to your word.

Hail Mary, etc.

V. And the Word was made flesh

R. And dwelt among us.

Hail Mary, etc.

V. Pray for us, O holy Mother of God.

R. That we may be made worthy of the promises of Christ.

Let us pray

Pour forth, we beseech you, O Lord, your grace into our hearts, that as we have known the Incarnation of Christ, your son by the message of an angel, so by his passion and cross, we may be brought to the glory of his resurrection, through the same Christ our Lord. Amen.

The Memorare

Remember, O most gracious Virgin Mary, that never was it known that any one who fled to your protection, implored your help, and sought your intercession, was left forsaken. Inspired with this confidence, I fly unto you, O Virgin of virgins, my mother; to you I come, before you I stand, sinful and sorrowful. O Mother of the Word Incarnate, despise not my petitions, but in your clemency hear and answer me. Amen.

The above prayers are taken from Way of life, the Catechism of Pope St. Pius X, translated by Msgr. Eugene Kevane, Center for Family Catechetics.

Mysteries of the Rosary

A. Joyful mysteries (Mon. & Thur.)

1. Gabriel's annunciation to Mary
2. Visit of Mary to cousin Elizabeth
3. Birth of Jesus in Bethlehem
4. Presentation of Jesus in the temple
5. Finding the child Jesus in the temple.

B. Sorrowful mysteries (Tue. & Fri.)

1. Jesus in the garden of Gethsemani
2. Scourging of Jesus
3. Crowning with thorns
4. Carrying of the cross to Calvary
5. Crucifixion and death of Jesus.

C. Glorious mysteries

1. Resurrection of Jesus
2. The Ascension of Jesus into heaven
3. Descent of the Holy Spirit upon Mary and the Apostles
4. Assumption of Mary into heaven
5. Crowning of Mary as Queen of heaven.